How to Survive Schizophrenia

By Mike Hedrick

1

<u>How to Ask for Help in a Crisis</u>

I have lived with schizophrenia for eleven years. In those eleven years I have gone through cycles of wellness and while it primarily gets better with each passing day, there are still periods here and there where life becomes too overwhelming or where I push myself too hard and then I feel the intense crushing weight of existence on my shoulders.

In those times I tend to retreat, not only to my apartment but into myself. I lay there on my couch staring at the TV, emotions flowing through my spine and it's all I can do not to keep myself from crying.

Sometimes the feeling lasts for only a day or two, other times it builds until there's a tipping point where I make some declaration of exasperation and throw my family into a tizzy of worry.

Yes it's been eight years, and yes I'm getting better at recognizing my moods and the way things are going but there are still nights where I would be ok if I didn't wake up in the morning.

In times like these it's important to find some kind of help, at the very least a kind ear to hear your problems or a shoulder to burrow into and let the tears trickle if that's what you need.

On hard nights you think, "I wish someone would just reach out to me, I wish someone would ask me how I'm doing. Why don't people care about me?" This is not a good series of inner voices.

I know what it's like to feel like no one cares about you. I know what it's like to feel like you're some defect in the algorithm of life but it's important to know that more people care about you than you realize.

There are people out there who would jump up at a moments notice to come to your aid, to give you a hug and to rub your back and tell you they love you.

You can't be afraid to ask for help when you need it, you can't be afraid to make a call to your mom or your dad or your brother or your sister or a close friend. How else are they supposed to know that you're having a hard time if you don't tell them?

I'm no stranger to wearing the "everything's ok" mask and then going home and crawling into a ball in your bed hoping to God that it would just end.

It can take a good deal of courage to make that call, it can take a crisis to make you take action in taking care of yourself and I know it's hard not to feel like your complaining is a bother to those around you. I know what's it like to feel like you have no outlet because you feel like a burden to those close to you.

All you have to do is pick up that phone though.

The good thing about family and friends is that no matter what you're going through, they'll be there to calm you down.

It's also important to recognize when a crisis may be coming. It takes years to get to know yourself well enough to realize the signs that you may need to take a break.

Ennui is defined as a feeling of listlessness and dissatisfaction arising from a lack of occupation or excitement. It's a dull feeling at first but it always comes on in the days or weeks before a crisis.

When I feel it I know it's time to start taking things a little easier and to stop being so hard on myself about things that I could've done differently. Learn to recognize ennui and you may able to avert a crisis by reaching out before it escalates into something you can't control.

It's also important to know that suicide is never the answer, whatever difficulties you have in life can be solved. Suicide is finality.

Don't be afraid to reach out if you need help. There are people that care about you whether you like it or not. You're ok and people love you, I promise.

2

The Importance of Having a Friend to Talk You Down

I'm stable. At least that's how I usually am.

In the eleven years I've lived with schizophrenia I've managed to find a pretty strong footing for my life. I take my meds and go to therapy and practice my social skills and hell, I even have a job, which is more than a lot of people with schizophrenia can handle.

That said, there are times where the stars align for madness and you lose yourself in being overwhelmed with feelings or thoughts that confuse and delude you.

This past week was one of those times for me.

I was so lost in a certain idea that I started to lose my grip on reality. It was almost like a sickness, a fever of the mind where no matter how hard I tried, no matter what I told myself, I could not shake this completely unrealistic idea.

To say it consumed me would be an understatement.

I suffered with this delusion for a good five days trying anything, meditation, self talk, even copious cigarettes to calm me down.

I was lost until two days ago when I struck up a conversation with a friend who's helped me with this type of stuff before. When she asked me how I was doing I couldn't help but unload and I told her everything, every gritty detail.

After some back and forth describing things more carefully she, in her unabashed way hit me with the truth, she described a thought I had had many times in my midst of delusion but her saying it out loud and, I guess, hearing it from another person, the thought finally started to put down roots in my mind.

In a matter of probably minutes I came to my senses and realized the reality of the situation.

The delusion was rooted in obsession and it simply wasn't realistic to pursue it any further.

I won't go into details because it's kind of a private matter but my point remains.

Sometimes you need to hear the truth from someone else for it to really stick.

I told her later that I realized I probably needed to hear what she said just to knock myself back down to reality.

Even though the exact thought had occurred to me numerous times during the week, the way she said it and probably the fact that she said it at all reinforced the idea that I had been reluctant to accept.

I was just being willfully ignorant of the truth and hearing it from another person, one that I love and trust as a very close friend helped me regain my grip on reality.

Essentially, we need friends to help us with stuff, if it's not help moving to a new place, it's bouncing an idea off of them and learning to see the situation from another person's point of view.

Good friends know you well, they know what sets you off and they know what needs to be said in order to calm you down.

Sometimes it's the blunt truth.

All said, I'm feeling better today, I don't feel quite so overwhelmed by this idea and I'm taking things slowly again.

Maybe it was because it's been a particularly stressful few weeks or maybe it was just, like I said, the stars aligning for a bit of madness.

I needed to hear the truth though and I needed to hear it from someone I trust. I'm thankful for that.

In essence, where would we be without friends? I know I'd probably be completely lost in my own mind.

3

You are not alone in your diagnosis of mental illness

In the time I've lived with schizophrenia I've seen horrible days and I've seen days where the sun seemed to shine just right on my face and strike a certain happiness in my soul.

Throughout everyday though, I've struggled with my thoughts.

There isn't a day that goes by where a bit of panic doesn't creep up into me. In those moments it can feel like the world is against you. It can feel like you are the only person alive who is feeling that certain kind of panic but I'm here to tell you that you're not.

Approximately 2.4 million American adults suffer with schizophrenia. That's a little more than 1% of the population of the U.S. and although 1% doesn't seem like a lot it's certainly more than can fit in one professional football stadium.

Sometimes I like to think about that when I'm having a bad day. I imagine myself standing in a crowd thousands who each know singularly what it's like to live with either debilitating paranoia or delusions.

These are people that are spread all across the U.S. in every small town and every place you've never been or never even thought of being.

1.1% percent of the population means that one in every hundred people has schizophrenia.

I like to think of it as some kind of special distinction and while I don't want to equate my delusions to reality, me and you and every other person with schizophrenia is the one person out of a hundred that God chose to touch.

The point I'm trying to make here is that you are never alone. Even when it feels like the world is crumbling in around you and you've lost hope for ever pulling yourself out of a particularly deep hole, it's pretty much guaranteed that there's another person out there, if not many that are in the exact same kind of hole.

I've been to numerous schizophrenia support groups like schizophrenia anonymous and while support groups are all fine and good, there's a certain air to them that feels competitive like you're trying to outdo everyone else in the group with the severity of your experience.

Instead, I've taken a liking to a certain chat room on the internet for people with schizophrenia. You can go into it without judgment because you don't see the other people. In essence it's just words being typed into a window.

Those words have connected me to more strongly to the experience of living with schizophrenia than any support group I've ever been to though.

There's something extremely freeing about not having to see the other people you're talking to.

In case you're interested and having a bad day and just want to talk the chat room is at http://theircvillage.com/chat/ .

It's hard to explain what talking to other schizophrenics is like when there's no judgment.

It's a window into an entirely different world of experiences. These are experiences that you thought you were alone in but in chat rooms such as this you realize that those experiences are part and parcel of the schizophrenia experience.

What's the point of all this? Just to let you know that if you're suffering you are not alone in what you're feeling and what you are experiencing. You never have been and you never will be. I feel comfortable making the guarantee that there's at least one other person in the world who is in the exact same spot.

I know my words may seem cliché but they are true and it's important to know that.

4

The Five Stages of Grief After A Diagnosis of Mental Illness

I've seen good days and horrible days, I've had successes and I've had failures but nothing can compare to the despair I felt in the first few months and years of living with the illness.

They say there are five stages of grief when you lose a loved one. I can tell you from personal experience that those five stages also exist and are just as intense when you're told you're crazy.

Instead of losing someone you loved you've lost yourself or at least your conception of yourself.

First there's denial, in my case I didn't believe my diagnosis, I thought "they're all playing a trick on me to make me think I'm crazy, it's all a ruse" I thought the psychiatrists office was a set up and I was so reluctant to accept the diagnosis that I couldn't even make it through a therapy session without storming out.

That segues into the second stage, anger. I was angry with my parents for taking me to the hospital and putting me through this, I was angry with myself for being affected by my thoughts and I was angry with the doctors who were trying to force me into a view of health I had yet to accept. If I was crazy, I was gonna get well on my own.

The third stage of grief is bargaining. Eventually I made the bargain halfway through my stay at the hospital that I'd take my meds if it would mean I could get out of there sooner. I made concessions with myself to stick with treatment until I could get out of the hospital and back to my own life.

Depression is the next stage. I can recall days where I was so sick and sad that I didn't want to get out of bed. It bothered me with every ounce of my being that my mind was still telling me these weird things, that it was still playing tricks on me even in the mental hospital where these things needed to go away. The depression lasted for a long time, even after I got out of the hospital I was in a daze, without hope for months after I got out, too tired to speak, too frustrated with med side effects. I just didn't want to deal with any of it. I stopped taking care of myself, I stopped caring about my health and gained weight and I was so bogged by delusions and paranoia that I preferred not to even go out into public.

The last stage of grief is acceptance, and like anything else it takes a great deal of time to get to that point. Acceptance is the point at which you say to yourself, "Ok, maybe the things I experience aren't real, maybe I actually am sick, after all there's no basis in reality for any of my beliefs and I've noticed that when I take my meds I seem to feel better, maybe there's actually something to this."

To accept things and move on and get better though, you need things like the intuition to realize you're sick, you need fear to motivate you to conquer it, and most of all you need hope that one day things will get better.

It's hard to find that hope in your darkest days but that's where pushing yourself and practice with the things that disturb you come in.

Say you have the irrational belief that everyone hates you, every time you interact with someone and it goes smoothly, and they're polite, you get a little boost of confidence and proof that what you believe isn't necessarily the truth.

Eventually hundreds of these pleasant interactions lead to thousands, which build a foundation for reality in your mind. As this foundation builds you start to see the light at the end of the tunnel and you start to feel a lot better about yourself.

In time you'll realize that your sickness is manageable. You will realize that a diagnosis doesn't define you.

I can guarantee that some symptoms will never go away but with this foundation of reality and hope they become a lot more manageable. At least that's how it worked for me.

5

Accepting a Mental Illness Diagnosis

I can remember when I was told that I was crazy. It was an apex in my life resulting from nearly two years of skewed thinking and symptoms so bad I could barely leave my house.

The diagnosis came three days into my week-long stay at the Boulder Community Hospital after a spur of the moment trip to the U.N. where I thought I was a prophet.

This trip held all the meaning in the world to me. It was my magnum opus, it was what I was put on the earth to do, and although I was apprehensive about being given the responsibility of bringing peace to the world, I carried out my mission to the best of my abilities.

There was one overarching thing I couldn't get past though, and that was the fact that every message I was getting from god didn't seem to have any concrete basis in reality, no tangible evidence that what I was being told was real.

Because of this, I had the suspicion that something might be wrong with me, but it didn't cement until the day I was told my diagnosis and my world crumbled. My grand status and everything I had experienced in the last year wasn't real. It was all in my head.

It's hard to accept the fact that you're sick. It's hard to face the world when you know that you're crazy. What's the point of getting bed in the morning if life is nothing but a series of days bleeding together where you're just an insignificant speck of dust? I had pinned everything on the notion that I was some kind of vastly important person, but I was wrong. I was just some insignificant crazy guy. What a bleak world.

For a long time afterwards I tried desperately to define myself amidst a daily struggle of paranoia and depression. I tried to be normal but I just didn't have the energy to put on that show. Instead I retreated into myself. I was unsure of who I was and how this diagnosis defined me.

For years I numbed the fear with pot and I chased the feeling of grandiosity I had once had, but I could never get a hold of it. I wanted to be someone important because in that first episode I was God and it felt good.

I'd like to say that there was a single definable point at which I accepted that I was sick and I accepted that getting better would take work but that would be a lie.

It took years of very gradual improvement and growing into the man that I am to get to a point of being comfortable with myself and with my diagnosis. It took frustration, exasperation, depression and thousands of days after days to grow into being ok with things. It took the realization that improvement takes work and it takes practice.

There isn't a set guide of principals I can share that will help someone accept their diagnosis and get better. It's different for each person.

Perhaps the one piece of advice I can give though is don't give up. Set a goal for yourself for how you want to be, for the type of person you want to be, and for how you want to be seen by the world and keep working at it.

For me, that goal was to be a normal, happy, confident man who could be easy in conversation and could relate to anyone.

I didn't let the illness define me and I didn't give up with accepting life that way.

I'd be lying if I said I wasn't still working toward that goal but I can say I've gotten pretty darn good at it and you wouldn't have any idea I had schizophrenia unless I told you.

The takeaway though? If you let your illness define you as a person and give up the fight for the life you want then there's not a good deal you can do to get better. If you work at it though, take your meds and constantly try to improve yourself and your situation, you can find your stability.

6

Finding healing in a regimented routine

I can remember the early days of having schizophrenia. For the first two or three years there was a lot to make sense of. Right out of the shoot I was experiencing delusions about what people were saying about me.

I was so afraid of the implications of subtle body language, from a lingering millisecond of eye contact to the way my feet hit the ground when I walked, to the way I was holding my hands to my side that it was a struggle to even go into a store or, really, anywhere I was bound to see another living member of the human species.

It wasn't just their opinions that meant so much, it was the numerous, many times confusing, many times confounding and many times contradictory underlying messages that they were projecting that buried me. This is a hard one to explain but with a simple scratch of the head someone could be telling me to go forward, that what I was doing was right or that they were acknowledging the symbolic crown on my head that made me a king or a prophet or whatever I thought I was. To put it lightly, it was a confusing time for me.

In the midst of all the anxiety and delusions it's not hard to imagine that I was having a tough time grasping normalcy.

Several months after my diagnosis I took a job at a small town newspaper as a reporter, the days were monotonous and confusing as I sat in on city council meetings covering issues related to the lowering water table and interviewing local business owners for small blurbs in the local section all the while wondering if I was uncovering some vague connections to international conspiracy. I would review the interviews and wonder what they meant by using the specific set of words they used, whether that was an indication of guilt or secrecy or some other strange thing they needed to confess.

The nights were altogether different, everyday coming home to my apartment I would smoke pot and either lay on my couch watching TV or go out to the bar and get so hammered that I couldn't walk.

Eventually I lost my job but that wasn't the catalyst for change.

I still my spent my nights getting drunk but the pot use creeped into the days and I spent my time ironically writing a blog about how to live a peaceful life. I knew for sure that millions of people, some in high places were reading my words and reconsidering their positions, I knew I was making the world a better place and I knew it was inevitable that I'd get a million dollar book deal and go on to give seminars to congressmen and presidents and I would have my hand in changing the world. These are what they call delusions of grandeur. The thing is, I was trying to give advice, I think mainly to myself to get a place I desperately wanted to be. It's hard to admit that the only time I felt relaxed was when I was drunk.

It all came to a head one night in July. I had been out drinking all night and in the haze I decided it would be a good idea to drive the two miles back to my apartment. This is something I had done several times before but it had never dawned on me that it was a serious deal. I was doing good, not swerving and only several blocks from my house when I saw flashing lights behind me.

What started as a trip to the bar to unwind ended with me calling my parents to bail me out of jail at 3 a.m.

The next year of my life would mean change.

Not least of the repercussions, my license was suspended so I moved back home to Boulder so that my Parents could drive me to my appointments and so it would be easier to get around.

The year was marked by daily calls to a center for random drug and alcohol testing, breathalyzers and urine tests with a strange man watching me pee, numerous hours of community service and alcohol recovery group therapy every Saturday morning at 10:00.

I'd be lying if I said it wasn't a dramatic shift to a routine that was horribly boring and so far removed from what I was doing before that it was hard to take.

During that time though, I quit smoking pot, I quit drinking and I got some of the best sleep I'd gotten since my diagnosis. Trips to the bar on Monday afternoons turned into extended hours at coffee shops where I finished my first novel and wrote some of the best material that's ever come out of me.

In the routine, I found that I never forgot to take my meds, I always got at least eight hours of sleep and for some strange reason I felt much more relaxed and was able to finally wrap my head around the diagnosis of schizophrenia. The meanings things had before started to fade and I began to see the world as a mostly random series of events with no connected overarching conspiracy plot.

I stopped using alcohol as a means to feel normal and began to work on accepting things and interacting with the world in a relaxed, easy manner. The routine of it shocked me out of my stupor and allowed me to finally focus on working myself back to health.

My story ended where so many stories of recovery do, back at a place of normality, back at a place where the biggest things in my life are now friends and family and work. Drugs, alcohol and schizophrenia are just passing thoughts, parts of a story that I no longer suffer with. I'm perfectly able to get one or two beers at a restaurant without desperately feeling like I need eight more just to feel normal and I can see the world as a cautiously friendly place where most people have good intentions and not everybody I see has a personal vendetta against me. I no longer get secret messages from the TV and radio and the connections I make in my head don't speak of some grand conspiracy. I know I'm not a prophet and to be honest, it's much easier that way.

How to Have Schizophrenia and Function Normally

Schizophrenia is a strange kind of fun. On the one hand your lapses into crippling paranoia and delusional thinking will give you the edge you need to be sharp and cutthroat in social and business interactions, after all if you think everybody's out to get you, you don't have to make friends which opens up a lot of room for focusing on your specific goals. On the other hand, these same lapses into crippling paranoia and delusional thinking will make you so lonely and fearful of the world around you that you won't even want to interact and will therefore have endless amounts of free time as you sit huddled in the corner of your dark studio apartment with a loaded glock ready to strike at even the most subtle sound emanating from your neighbor's apartment.

This article is of course satire and attempting to make light of a horrible situation the subject of which I'm allowed to joke about because I've had schizophrenia for eight years. In it, I'll guide you through the steps of accepting your tragic fate and fighting to overcome it and one day having a semblance of functioning normally in society.

1. The diagnosis

This will be a shock to your system. The knowledge that you have an incurable brain disorder and must take powerful antipsychotic medication everyday for the rest of your life will seem like some insurmountable obstacle that shatters not only your dreams but your relationships with your friends and family.

The most important thing to remember here is that the quickest way to get out of the hospital is to comply and take your meds and go to your therapy groups. If the doctors see that you're compliant and are willing to accept your diagnosis as a sickness and not some divine ordination from the mouth of God you will get to go home sooner.

2. Delusions and Paranoia

When you get out of the hospital you will still be dangerously psychotic and you will still think that the whole operation was a set up or a ruse to keep you from discovering the secrets of the corrupt new world order. You will also be on constant guard from perceived threats like the way that one guy looked at you or that inflection in your friend's voice that signaled something that you are sure was an accusation.

Hopefully, the fact that all of this paranoia and these delusions you have about you being the second coming of Jesus Christ will seem, at the very least, a bit far fetched, even for you. The hope is that this realization will spark the realization that you actually are dangerously ill. That or the paranoia will be so invasive that you'll do anything to get it to go away. This is when you should think that maybe, if you keep taking your pills you might feel a bit better.

3. The Side Effects

You will get fat, you will have the feeling that you want to tear your skin off and that you can't sit still. You will feel extremely sedated and you will feel like taking your own life but don't fret, all of this is par for the course. Sometimes it takes years to get the right cocktail of meds and life will be hell in these areas for some time but on the plus side, your paranoia will lessen, your delusions will disappear and you will stop thinking that you're receiving secret messages from the television and radio.

Eventually, you will get on the right meds and get used to the side effects and accept them as part of your life.

4. Interacting With People Without Seeming Crazy

At some point along the way, you'll start to feel OK. You will never feel awesome but you will feel at least a bit better. This is called stability and once you reach that point you will want to improve even more. Part of improving is learning to interact with society without seeming crazy.

This takes several years to master and you must always be watching, evaluating, and analyzing your and other people's social interactions. If something didn't quite feel smooth or fluid and normal keep trying until it does, keep experimenting with different forms of eye contact, word inflection, and laughter until it becomes second nature. It will be hard but if you keep a sense of humor about it there's nothing stopping you.

5. How to get by without alienating your loved ones

During your recovery you will feel impulses to say and do things that are not normal. This is partly a result of feeling frustration that you are not acting normal, getting laid or getting anywhere personally and professionally, and that you are taking cues from an unreal and inflated view of the world that comes to you through television and movies. It's important to know that people don't actually act like you see them acting in the media.

The best thing to do in these situations is to try to learn to relax and interact in a sort of flow, or how it seems easiest to interact. If you force it, it won't feel normal. If you sit back and just let it happen naturally, you will have less of a learning curve and will already be better at interacting than most.

6. Being a normal human being

Once you have become stable, and have mastered the art of social interaction you can start to think about actually living a normal life. You can start thinking about getting a job or finding a relationship, this will be hard at first but just use what you've learned and expound on it in whatever way you can to get to a place you want to be.

Be warned, your diagnosis will be a detriment that you will have to live with and it may cause you to miss opportunities because of ignorance on society's part. You will have to deal with the stigma that people think you're going to shoot up a school or do something equally horrible but if you demonstrate in every facet of your life that you are still a good, nice, humble person and that your diagnosis isn't any different than having cancer or AIDS people will treat you with dignity and respect.

At least that's how it worked with me. Good luck and Godspeed!

8

Separating reality from delusion when you have a mental illness

In the midst of my most intense psychotic episode I thought I was a prophet.

I thought it was my job and my job alone to bring peace to the world.

I was receiving hidden messages that only I could see when I listened to the radio or watched television and I thought there was great evil coming to the world.

The clincher is, though, that although I was thinking all of this stuff, there was never any concrete tangible evidence that any of it was real.

At every turn my delusions that things were happening were rebuffed by everyday life.

Just one example was the hidden meaning I'd see in street signs that told me something, or told me to go somewhere, once I acted on that meaning though I was still just as lost as ever.

Everything that I thought held a hidden meaning was just a random turn of events. It was for this reason that the notion resided in me that I might very well may be sick.

It takes a good deal of effort and experience to separate the things your brain is telling you from the fact of reality. It takes time to realize that reality is in fact quite boring compared to your delusions.

I wish I could say that there was a definitive key for discerning what's real and what's not but if there is I haven't found it yet.

When you're sick, messages come from the strangest places, if not street signs with hidden meanings, it's people.

When you're sick you discern meaning and messages from the things people say, from the inflections in their voice and from the way they move.

It can come in the way they scratch their nose or tap their feet or look a certain direction or even the way they smile.

Of course each of these different movements may mean something entirely different when you're sick and it depends on the individual who's interpreting the movements.

Generally though, none of it means anything, especially to you.

It takes time to figure out that people are generally nice and that, to put it bluntly, they're pretty self absorbed, for them to spend time trying to send you a covert message would require knowledge on their part that you are an extremely important person or a spy and it would require training by some governmental agency as to what certain movements mean.

It would also require them executing those movements at a very precise time when you're looking.

That sounds pretty unrealistic doesn't it? Well it is.

The truth of the matter is that nobody is sending you any messages and if they were, at some point, your following these messages would pay off, but it never does.

Reality is boring. That's the simple truth. But it's a good kind of boring. It's a boring where you don't have to worry that people are talking about you or sending you messages or anything like that and in all honesty that's really quite freeing.

As I said before though, knowledge about what's real and what's not comes with the experience of living with a mental illness. It comes when you've lived through enough circumstances of seeing things as the boring everyday situations that they are without some grand meaning.

Meds help too. The meanings fade and you realize that you're just one person among the 7 billion on earth living your own life.

Accepting that you are not that important is nice. No longer do you have to worry about making an amazing impression on the world stage as the one true god or the second coming of Jesus. You are just you, plain old simple you.

9

On Human Interaction

Awkwardness is one thing. Panic is an entirely different animal. When one feeds into another there's the possibility for trouble.

Considering even the tiniest amount of eye contact, humans interact with one another hundreds of times a day, (and it's funny that I say 'humans' as if I don't belong to the species, which may be fitting considering how I feel a lot of the time).

There's so much room for error when it comes to interacting with any other person. What's strange though is how I classify error as something which is detrimental and traumatic and catastrophic to a conversation when it really isn't that big of a deal. The emphasis I place on getting a conversation 'right' and not appearing as anything other than a confident 28-year-old man is, to put it lightly, an exercise for me. It baffles me why I'm so concerned with controlling how another person perceives me. I don't want to get hurt though. I don't want to do something that would cause someone to say something negative about me. I don't want them to make fun of the way I act and then cause me to go on a many years long identity crisis about what it means when I act a certain way. I have a feeling that's just the paranoia talking though.

The thing is, when you have paranoid schizophrenia and think that everyone is out to harm you by making fun of you, there's a weird space you have to inhabit. This is a space where you have to have a hyper-awareness of every tiny thing that's happening around you, constantly reading the situation and the notions implied from things as small as involuntary muscle movements and body language to the words that are being said, in order to analyze if these things are an affront to the way you're acting or even looking.

It's hard, I'll say that.

To have the consistent nagging analysis running in your head about everything that's being said or maybe implied, and then to top that off with the attempt to appear normal, or as close to normal as possible, is something that, although purely schizophrenic, takes a great deal of mental aerobics.

It's easy to see that considering all that, there's a reason I'd prefer to stay at home in my comfortable chair with some soft music than to be out in public anywhere, where the possibility of interacting with another human being is inherently in the cards.

I say I'm an introvert for a reason.

Still though, there will always exist that urge to be close to someone, to love someone, to have that someone where I don't have to think about these things and instead can be free to be the weirdo I am naturally.

To get to that point though, a level of trust has to be established. This is essentially a trust so deep that nothing I do or that she does will be questioned with an ulterior motive. It's a trust that exists among mostly only brothers or sisters or children and parents. It's an undeniable trust that the things you do will have no effect that can offset the notion that these two people are intrinsically tied together through blood and will never be separate no matter what happens.

Some people refer to this as unconditional love and to make it with someone, anyone out there who is not already a part of your family takes an intense honesty that can only be made through the deepest levels of human interaction. Interaction that I have yet to achieve.

I imagine that level of trust is hard for anyone, especially without the basis of a years-long relationship. Building something like that though, seems to be an essential.

It requires a level of self-esteem and self awareness, at least enough to be able to have a conversation with another human being without flipping out.

Thus far I've had pretty good results. You wouldn't know I'm schizophrenic if I didn't tell you, I'm almost confident in saying that there may be no way of knowing if you talked to me. You can't sense the nerves in my voice and in my expression that were once there, but that's only because I'm ok with not being perfect. I still worry about it, but it doesn't consume me like it used to. I feel like there's still room for improvement. I still have a mini panic attack when I'm talking to people I don't know but It doesn't eat me. These mini panic attacks are now a routine part of my day. They must be dealt with just like one must brush their teeth, and one must shower. That's not to say I would prefer not to experience them at all.

I want to be good. I want to be able to go about my day without worrying about how someone perceives my actions but for now I can only do one thing. That is to accept that I can't control what people think about me. It's to accept that people may not like me.

I'm working on it.

10

<u>The importance of a strong support structure after a diagnosis
of mental illness</u>

When I was diagnosed with schizophrenia eight years ago it was like walking in a fog. I was lost in my delusions, I was confused about what was happening to me and I was trying to grapple with what exactly reality was.

My family was suffering too.

They had no background with mental illness and no frame of reference about what to expect with it.

I had asked for help a few times but they just thought my skewed thinking was a result of smoking marijuana and that once I stopped everything I would be fine. It didn't click for them until after my first major episode when they took me to the hospital and I was finally diagnosed.

I don't recall a whole lot from those first few months but I'm sure my parents were racking their brains for an answer about what to do with their son. It was even disclosed to me later on that my mom had sought anti-depressants because she was so concerned.

The case with a lot of instances of major mental illness is that the person who is sick doesn't realize or doesn't accept their illness and so they don't seek help. They refuse to take their meds and they refuse to go to the doctor.

Many times too, the family of the person who is sick has no clue about how to help, that or the family doesn't care or just plain isn't there. That's why a good deal of mentally ill people end up on the streets. The support structure just isn't there and to be honest, that breaks my heart.

I have been extremely fortunate to have a family that cared enough to educate themselves on what was going on. I can remember one day my Mom came home with an armload of books on mental illness and how to deal with it and she poured through those books voraciously, trying desperately to understand how to help.

Although I was a bit lost during that time, I was also fortunate to understand and realize that what was happening in my brain wasn't right. I think those two factors can make or break recovery.

Someone has to want to recover and there needs to be a support structure in place to aid the person in their recovery.

Not long after my diagnosis my parents enrolled in NAMI's Family-to-Family support group and class and it was reiterated to them that the most important thing they can do is have patience.

So many families give up on their mentally ill members when the going gets tough and I can tell you, the going will get tough.

It's important for a family to stick it out though and ride the waves because in time, their son or daughter or brother or sister will improve. It will be a long, slow, many times painful process but the family at the other end of recovery will be so much stronger for it.

Even in cases where the mentally ill family member refuses to accept to accept that they're sick, the thing they want most is an ear to listen and a shoulder to cry on.

If a family is patient with their son, and talks to him with a kind heart, an understanding tone and most of all love, the son will know that he can trust someone, and when you don't know the difference between reality and your own delusions being able to trust someone is perhaps the most important factor in recovery.

It's ok to be scared when a family member is ill but with patience and understanding even in the face of fear, there's a good chance you can bring your family member back from the brink.

I'm under no illusions that I myself might be out there wandering the streets were it not for the support and understanding my family gave me in my most tumultuous times.

Together we navigated not only the illness, but the options that were available to me with meds, benefits and wellness and eight years on, I'm a regular columnist at PsychCentral.com and The New York Times.

It will be hard to be there for your family member but it will be worth it.

11

How I learned to stop worrying

Where should I start? It's been a rough few years. For a long time, I had no idea who I was. I was lost in a fog of worry about what people thought and what exactly made me the man I was.

I was diagnosed with schizophrenia when I was 20 years old. It was a tough pill to swallow, especially when I was unaware if what I was experiencing was actual reality.
It's been eight years since then, in that time I've worked and I've worked hard to climb up to some, any tangible ledge of stability. I've questioned myself millions of times over and wondered if the things that were happening in my mind had any real basis in the real world. Sometimes they have, most of the time they haven't.

Somewhere along the line, I decided church might be a good option. The people seemed like good honest people, people that wouldn't judge you unfairly for some character flaw or some tiny thing I imagined people were judging me for.

Before then I had all but completely rejected any idea of God from my life, I had taken my faith from science but as amazing and logical and thought provoking as it was, it was an empty faith. It was a faith that didn't allow me to feel like I was a part of something, a faith that didn't allow me to feel protected and most of all, forgiven if I did something I wasn't proud of.

It was strange at first, seeing these people who put their stock in something I wasn't sure was even there but they were strong people, earnest and accepting and it seemed like they knew something I didn't. It seemed like they had some power behind their fight, something to fall back on besides themselves, and I wanted that.
I went into a twenty-something group and they spoke about a richness of faith and a personal journey that seemed although persecuted, extremely fulfilling. It was something I could barely even imagine, but I went in with open arms.

The truth was though, I had no idea how to act around these people. This is assuming I had to act at all, but I knew that I was in a place they couldn't understand. I simply didn't know what was expected of me and my behavior here in this group of people, should I talk to them like I talked to my friends, swearing and carrying on, or should I try to be the way they seemed.
I've never really fit in anywhere but I've made friends and I've found a niche in the world that allows me to do the things I want to do. I don't think I fit in there at the church group but you don't need that community to have a certain kind of faith. All said though, I did take something with me.

That thing was the possibility that there was someone or something big out there that had my back when I doubted myself.

I've seen a lot of worry in my life, I've seen countless periods of depression, rejection and paranoia and a lot of those times I felt completely alone. I would be completely consumed by these feelings and hope evaporated. I'd be lying if I hadn't considered ending things but I knew that I couldn't. If not least for my family who would miss me with an unending ferocity.

Since those few brief weeks in the twenty-something group though, I've opened up to the possibility of God. I ask for help when I need it and when I feel overwhelmed and I express gratitude when something happens that doesn't seem like I did it myself. You can call it luck, but I like to think maybe there was some spiritual intervention.

I have a kind of faith that serves me well. It's a private faith, and it's one I keep to myself but it helps me through the tough times. It gives me a peace of knowing that I have help in this universe, even if I don't need it.
It's given me something to put my problems, my worries and my anxieties in and trust that what's supposed to happen will happen and what isn't, won't.

It was tough for me to accept things at first, but all it really takes is a simple phrase coming from a whisper as you lay your head on the pillow. "Lord I trust you, guide me to where I need to be."

The deep breath and the loosening of your shoulders alone after you say the words is worth it, and I'd be lying if I said saying it hasn't become a nightly ritual to help me fall asleep.

I don't know where I am in terms of a "spiritual journey" at this point. I just know that I have God backing me up and the comfort I get from that knowledge is about all I need.

We all have things we worry about. Whether you like it or not though, there's something out there that's willing to take the burden and loosen the load, to put your trust into if you can't put it anywhere else. There is something that has your back in this world and to take that chance and accept the help is transformative.

12

Daily Life with Schizophrenia

I'm here, I showed up. That's about the extent of my abilities when it comes to living with schizophrenia. I can't say I'll be engaged but I'm here and I'm taking life on, day by day, minute by minute.

I've lived with this illness for nine and a half years and the days, that were once quite chaotic, have kind of devolved into a set routine that, although seemingly boring to some, gives me a stability that I treasure.

Most days are the same, wake up, bagel and coffee, then to the coffee shop to get my work done, then lunch, then I have the afternoons free and most days I just go home and read or browse the internet. It's a simple routine, and it's reliable and though at times it feels stagnant, I like the predictability.

The sameness of it all gives me a pretty solid foundation because I know that at some point during the day, something will happen that will trigger my paranoia. Usually it has something to do with people. It's been labeled as social anxiety or introversion or any number of other things but dealing with people is hard for someone in my situation. Even if it's just a barista or a cashier, my mind will be reeling as I try to force out the correct words in the correct sequence with the correct body language and the correct eye contact, and as you can imagine, sometimes I get distracted.

Other times it's people I don't even interact with but who are sharing the same space and I'm hyper aware of any potential ridicule or criticism because of my paranoia, so at times, I can't really sit still. Sometimes it's overheard laughter, sometimes it's the look of someone, sometimes it's an eavesdropped word that starts a cycle in my brain of obscure persecutory meanings.

These little triggers will start compounding into a cycle where my mind is telling me that I'm being made fun of, that people are laughing about me or that I'm doing something weird.

I'll sit in the paranoia for a while until it either subsides or it gets to be too much in which case I'll leave and go outside for a cigarette. Most of the time the paranoia levels off and I can continue with my day but some days it gets so bad that my mind starts to buzz and my eyes get itchy. Too much input like a child crying loudly, or too much traffic, or a crowd of people sets off the cycle too so I'm careful about that stuff when for anyone else, it's just a momentary inconvenience. When I get home, I feel like my main fuse has blown, I just feel burnt. I can't focus on anything and I have no choice in the matter but to lay on my couch and close my eyes or just zone out on some innocuous science show on TV.

I like to keep things quiet too, the volume on my music and on the TV are low because the din has a way of calming me. If things get too loud I get anxious.

I realize this all sounds exhausting to deal with but it's life, and most days are pretty good, I have the freedom to do what I want and I'm content. It's my day to day and I've gotten pretty good at controlling everything so it's just right. I don't let the triggers control me, as I've gotten older and more experienced with schizophrenia I've learned to accept a lot of things at face value which prevents me from dwelling on superfluous details.

Save for the paranoia, I'm happy, I can handle life the way I've made it and things are manageable.

That's the way I like to keep it.

13

Paranoia Doesn't Take a Vacation

Last weekend I went camping. It was a needed respite after a few weeks of feeling incredibly stagnant and depressed. It was time I needed to get away.

We set up in a campground that seemed nice, there was a gorgeous lake view, there were plenty of trees and we had a campfire that made everything great and it was serene.

That is, until the neighbors showed up. They looked some rough people, ranchers or rednecks with little sensitivity. It's hard to determine why some people trigger my paranoia, they could've been great people but there was just something about them that didn't sit right with me.

As the afternoon carried on I'd catch laughter from them, snippets of conversation that I'd string together into persecution and then the nasty devil on my shoulder that brought everything together into a storm. In all likelihood, they were probably, most assuredly not even paying attention to me but the stew in my head was boiling and because of that I felt nervous, anxious and on edge which is not something you want to feel when you're on a camping vacation.

Warily, I told my parents what I was feeling and though it brought a bit of an edge to an otherwise peaceful afternoon, they talked me down and I took my meds and in a matter of time I felt ok.

There was still a bit of bite any time I sat outside and could see them though, and though I dealt with it, I wish I didn't have to.

That's the thing about schizophrenia though, it never takes a vacation. Despite all your efforts to limit stress there's always something that could trigger your symptoms, even when you're on vacation.

I wish I didn't have to deal with this stuff and I have to admit I got choked up when my dad told me that he and my mom wished they could take the illness on themselves instead of me having to deal with it.

That's life with a mental illness though, you never know when your symptoms could show up and because of that, you have to be prepared. You have to have your mental tricks and people that understand at the ready in case you need to work through it. There are so many opportunities for your symptoms to flare up and you have to be cognizant of the circumstances and people that trigger things. If you have to, it's ok to escape too.

All that said, I'm not sure our camping neighbors had any ill will whatsoever and this being a civil society I would hope that they didn't but that doesn't change the fact that the voices in my head started to say things that upset me in that moment.

I've been dealing with this stuff for almost ten years now though so even if I get caught up in it, I'm ready for everything it can throw at me.

You have to be if you live with this stuff.

14

Facing Stigma As a Person with Schizophrenia

I was diagnosed with schizophrenia ten years ago. In that time, I've been able to stabilize mostly and regain a sense of self that was all but lost in the first few years I was sick.

As a writer, the next challenge is always, "What should I write about?" and to say the least, schizophrenia has given me so much to put on the page.

There are so many different challenges and facets that someone with schizophrenia experiences that to cover everything I'd have to fill a library.

I won't lie that the illness is also a blessing though, writing about my experiences has gotten me bylines in some of the most prestigious publications out there and it's provided a basis for self sufficiency.

It's fair to say that at this point, the illness doesn't really bother me.

There's one facet of living with a mental illness that never goes away though, or won't until the general public is at least a bit more educated about what it's like to live this way.

That facet is the stigma each and every one of us who are sick faces in society.

It's been said time and again that the media perpetuates this stigma and that's because it's the truth.

When was the last time there was a major tragedy in this country where the stability of the mental health of the perpetrator wasn't called into question?

The fact that that stability is even brought up is an unfortunate consequence of the never ending news cycle as the media looks for any story imaginable to try to explain the reasoning behind the tragedy.

Sadly, many times the mental health of the perpetrator is, in fact, suspect though, and that only fuels the stigma.

The overwhelming truth is that those with a major mental illness are much more likely to be victims of violent crime rather than perpetrators.

Maybe if the media spent more time focusing on some of the intensely creative and sensitive lives that people with mental illness live, things would be better. Sadly the media hasn't yet done that.

I see it everyday of my life when I have to tell people what I do for a living. I tell them I write, they ask me what I write about, I tell them I write about mental health and then comes the inevitable question, why? If I choose to tell them I live with schizophrenia their eyebrows raise and the next thing out of their mouth, if they are not speechless is "Wow." Or "But you seem so normal."

I can remember a date I went on where the topic came up and the girl asked me outright if I had ever killed anybody.

The truth is, stigma is out there. It has the potential to pop up anytime the subject is broached and when there is a mass shooting almost every week in this country the subject is broached quite a lot.

I'd be lying if I said it didn't bother me but at this point, I've come to expect that if I go there, I may get a reaction that isn't what I hoped for.

As I said earlier, I think the only thing that can change the thinking behind mental illness for anyone who has no experience with it is education.

That's one of the reasons I write about it for a living.

Hopefully through my words and my experience, the reality that we suffer with this will be more widely known.

In my case I share so much about mental illness with my friends family and followers that at this point, it's become kind of old and I hope that's a good thing.

I hope that if any of the hundreds of people I interact with regularly ever come across an instance of mental illness they'll think, "Oh, my friend Mike has schizophrenia, he's a great guy." Then they won't be so hesitant about the situation.

We are normal people, as far as the word normal takes us, we just have a little trouble with our thoughts.

It's an illness as far as cancer or diabetes is an illness but until the media finds something else to speculate about the stigma will be present. It's a shame, but just remember that there are people out there like your friends, your family and organizations like Bring Change to Mind that understand.

The truth is, you're not without friends.

15

On Depression

I feel like I should open this essay with a grand sweeping phrase that encompasses the enormity of life. It would be something like "Life is a mystery" or "The world is too big" but those don't seem to fit for some reason.

Those things are true though, the world is too big and life is indeed a mystery but to correctly express the feeling of it all one would have to gather every circumstance and every tiny thing in their life and write a volumes long, at times quite boring, yet ultimately fascinating tome on the whole thing and I fear even that wouldn't even begin to scratch the surface of the tip of the iceberg.

We all have times, though, when it gets to be too much. When the enormous intensity of being human draws out of us that last inkling of stability. We all break at some point or another. It may come at the end of a long week, one where the only thing on your mind was the intense dissatisfaction with your place in the world, the overwhelming and nagging notion that you needed to escape but you couldn't. Maybe because of this feeling you went out drinking with the guys to let off some steam but really the only steam you let off was your dwindling energy for putting up with things. You just feel tired. So tired. Maybe tired isn't even the right word but that's the one you tell everybody because no other word comes close to describing how you feel.

You just want the winter to come because when it snows, you can put up the hood on your sweatshirt, you can hide under the blankets, and it's quiet. Dead quiet. And when you go out on your deck for a cigarette at 2 a.m. you can hear the blood rushing in your ears but little else. The snow falls silently but gracefully and you know for the first time in a long time it feels nice. You are alone here and now and you can finally think.

We all have anxieties. There are times when we all think just too damn much and we wish the brain rattling around in our skull would just, please, shut the fuck up. It's true you've had fun in your life and you know what it feels like, but the idea of being around your friends at this moment sickens you for some reason. It's just all too much.

You need to know though. That it's ok to feel like that.

It's ok to feel the immense frustration with your efforts at life and to just want close up shop and not converse with anyone for days.

It's ok to not want any of it anymore.

It's ok to be alone and to think and to be frustrated. No one should feel guilty for being depressed. You may feel like a burden to those who are closest but in that period of nothingness, the ones who stick around are the ones who are worth it.

The human condition is a multifaceted tapestry of ups and downs, lefts and rights, loose threads and stitching mistakes. There are times when the one mistake you made sits there and glares at you and you keep staring at it hoping somehow you could make it go away or you undo the entire row of stitching to get at it but it's already too mired and it can't be corrected.

What makes a person though is whether they decide to keep stitching despite the blemish. Soon the row is finished and then the next ten rows are finished and you look at the thing and it's pretty nice even with the blemish there.

I've often told my friends who are suffering that the easiest but bravest thing one can do in those periods is to just keep waking up in the morning. Keep opening your eyes and if you have to lay on the couch all day waiting for bedtime just keep doing it.

Time will pass and when you're ten rows down the line you can look at your life and realize that although there was that one glaring blemish, the rest of it looks pretty good.

Everyone has blemishes in their life, even the ones who seem to have it all together. They may hide it better but they exist just as presently floating on the sweeping up and down waves of life.

You're ok. Just know that.

It's ok to want to be alone. It will be ok when you don't.

16

How to be Resilient

I've been living with schizophrenia for about nine years now. In that time, I've been subject to intense crippling moments of depression, paranoia and delusions. There have been times when it's gotten so bad I just about broke.

I've thought about killing myself more times than I can count and I'd be lying if I said it hasn't been a struggle.

I know what it's like to lie awake in bed at night, staring at the ceiling, brain buzzing, feeling like you can't breathe because it's just gotten to be too much.

Eventually though, sleep finds you and in the morning, things usually don't seem as bad.

My stability has been shaken more times than I can count but every single earthquake I've sat through has helped me fix the faults that were there before and has allowed me to build a foundation that can weather anything.

Love can shake the foundation, depression can shake the foundation and paranoia and delusions can shake the foundation.

The main thing is though, that that stuff passes, it may take weeks or months but eventually the hard stuff fades.

That's resiliency.

It's the simple act of sitting still and waiting for things to pass.

I realize that while you sit still and wait you may feel as if you want to claw your eyes out, that your heart feels like it's going to explode and spiders of invasive thoughts may be crawling across your skin and face but if you just sit still and wait, just go through the motions on autopilot and just keep waking up in the morning, the nastiness will fade and you'll eventually feel ok again.

There's always the advice of accepting the circumstances radically to ease the fight mechanism, to embrace the nastiness for all it's worth and sit with it and grow comfortable with it.

That helps but it will still be there.

Faith, although sometimes looked down upon can help too. Believing in something greater, a plan, the universe, God or whatever can slow your breath and give you a moment to relax as you feel the weight.

The crux though, is that you have to sit still and wait and wait and wait until the pain starts to fade because I can promise you that it will.

It will be a long slow process but sitting through it will give you strength, it will prove to you how mighty you are to be able to take it without breaking.

My friend once remarked to me that life is a river and we're on a raft floating down it, there will be rapids and there will be turns but if you spend enough time on the river you'll eventually become a guide and will be able to navigate those rapids and turns with stability and grace.

The point is, I know what it's like to have the stability you've worked so hard on to be shaken and to watch it crumble, you will climb back up though and find a much more stable foundation on which to sit and watch the world do what it does.

Stay strong, you can take this. It will be over soon.

17

It's ok if you can't do what normal people can do

In the last nine years since I was diagnosed I've worked hard to appear as normal as possible and to not let my schizophrenia define who I am and what I can do.

Still though, there are some things that remain outside of my capabilities as a disabled person.

Here's how it goes, I get an idea of what I want to happen and then I work feverishly on that idea until it either comes to fruition or I run myself so hard that I inevitably hit a wall. The wall is essentially the limit of stress I can endure before I start to feel myself slip backwards either by becoming depressed or more paranoid. Sometimes I don't realize that I've hit the wall until it's too late and I'm entrenched in thoughts of suicide or terrified by delusions. Finally, I'll realize that I just don't have it in me to accomplish what I want to accomplish and I'm forced to take a few days to a week to recover and get stable again.

I can only imagine that that's true for a lot of people in my situation.

The leader of my old schizophrenics anonymous group kept reiterating to me that you can't hold yourself to the same standards that normal people do, and while that seems a bit defeatist, it's taken me nine years to realize that that is true for a lot of the things in my life.

It's been a long course of testing my abilities and realizing where my limits lie. Realizing where your limits are though is something everyone has to come to terms with, schizophrenic or not, it's just that sometimes living with a mental illness makes your limits a little lower than normal people's.

I'm not saying you shouldn't try to achieve amazing things because you definitely should. I'm just saying that when you have a mental illness you need to be realistic about how much you can do without making yourself sick again.

I'd be lying if I said I didn't set extremely high standards for myself and I'm much harder on myself than I need to be and those two things have allowed me to do incredible things but the fact remains that I continue to hit the wall when I push myself too hard.

The fact of the matter is that it's ok if you can't do what normal people can do. It's ok if you can't achieve the same things that a person without mental illness can. To hold yourself to that same standard is unfair to you because you have an illness and a disability that puts limits on you whereas normal people don't.

At the same time, you shouldn't be too easy on yourself either and you shouldn't be lazy using your illness as an excuse.

If you can't conceivably do something without making yourself sick though it's probably a good idea to lower your expectations a little bit. It doesn't mean you can't achieve incredible things though, you just have to learn to take it slow and steady and slowly chip away at something and if you keep working at it you can do whatever you put your mind to.

Don't work yourself into the ground though if it's going to exacerbate your symptoms.

Success can wait however long it needs to in order for you to do the work you need to do at the pace you're comfortable with.

18

How to help a friend who's going crazy

It usually presents itself with a furrowed brow. Maybe the eye contact isn't the same as it used to be. Jokes don't come easy and the conversation is hard. There's something wrong and you just want things to be the way they used to.

I can remember a time when I was lost. I wasn't there. I had sunk into heavy drug use as a way to cope and if I hadn't outright insulted my closest friends, I had alienated them. Most of it was a downward shifting demeanor but part of it was the fact that I had been diagnosed with a serious mental illness.

There's truth in the notion that something like that scares people, they don't know what to do or how to help and for those suffering, it seems to be an endless haze of confusion about how to act or just generally how to be a human being.

Anybody who has a friend or family member with mental issues most definitely has a good share of horror stories and looking back on that time for myself, now that I'm amidst a relative stability, it doesn't seem real.

To say that I've separated myself from the person I was in the early stages would be an understatement but I've also embraced it and in my recovery I've come to recognize what exactly it takes to help somebody in those types of situations; especially if you're a friend.

The first thing a friend needs to know is that their buddy is still in there somewhere. They're just lost somewhere in the frightening thoughts. Imagine if every waking moment you were afraid that people's main motivations were at best, to make a fool out of you, or at worst hurt or kill you. Of course you'd be different. At that point the notion of even leaving one's house is too daunting to imagine, let alone going out to get a beer. Still, the fun loving friend that seemed to devolve into this fearful shell of fear and security is still in there and they desperately want to come out, they're just too afraid of what you'll think if they do.

The next thing a friend needs to know to help is what exactly their friend is experiencing. The best way to do that? Ask. What's their diagnosis? What's going on? What's it like? Don't be afraid to sit down and have a good talk with your friend to figure out what they're thinking or what's going on in their head. Your friend will be happy to unload because, if you do ask, it's likely the first time anybody has done so and everyone needs to take a load off at some point.

Don't be alarmed if what your friend says scares you or seems completely irrational, I can pretty much guarantee it will. In that vein, don't try to tell them what's real or argue with them, because what's real to them may be completely out of the realm of rational thought. Just fucking listen. Let them unload. Then, if you feel so inclined, educate yourself. Learn about the illness and understand that this behavior is not isolated to your friend; millions experience mental illness.

Just be a good friend. That is, be there for them.

Understand that your friend who may have been a different person in high school, is going through, to put it in the simplest terms, a rough time. This rough time may last for years or it may never end but it doesn't mean that your friend is gone. They're just different now. There may come a day, if your friend is diligent with their recovery, when things will seem closer to normal and you feel like things are better. Understand though, that there is no cure for mental illness, it is chronic and it will be a part of your friend from here on out.

Really though, the best thing you can do for them is to just keep being their friend. Don't treat them differently than you ever would have, because they will know and that will make them feel worse. Don't gossip to your other friends that you're friend is insane because gossip and speculation is the last thing that a paranoid schizophrenic needs to experience. It only serves to reinforce the irrational fear that people are out to get them.

A concern among mental health professionals is the fact that many people who are suffering isolate themselves and forego human contact. When you're afraid and panicking every minute of the day about what others are thinking, or doing to you it's completely understandable that you'd want to isolate yourself, and get away from the evils of society. That's why it's more important than ever to be a friend. Let them know they're not alone and that you have their back.

Out of all that though, just be there for them. That's pretty much the only thing that they really truly need.

Your friend may do something that scares you but it's important to know that they're only doing it because their thoughts have convinced them that there's no other choice. It may be hard to remain friends after that but if you do, you'll be rewarded with some of the best conversations, the richest experiences, and the deepest level of friendship that might ever possible, because you stuck around and no one else did.

19

Little things aren't a big deal when you have a mental illness

One thing that I'm continually amazed by is the fact that things that were once a huge deal before I was diagnosed practically became little more than minor inconveniences after living with a mental illness long enough.

These include things like rejection, opportunity loss, breakups, bad days, pretty much anything that has the potential to set someone off.

The weird thing is, you realize none of it really matters after living with a mental illness because practically anything the world manages to throw at you pales in comparison to the constant day-in day-out struggle of being able to trust your own mind.

Last week I got pretty sick with a nasty cold and for a normal person it would've knocked them out and put them completely out of commission physically and mentally. While it did take a toll on me physically, it wasn't nearly as bad mentally as some of the paranoia and delusional thinking I go through on a regular basis.

Maybe that's because I knew I would come out of it. I knew that in a week's time I would be feeling better and I just had to power through.

The same can't be said for mental illness, I know I'll never get rid of the paranoia and depression and delusions completely and there's a much heavier burden about something that can't be fixed.

That's where the resilience comes from though, that's where you realize that the symptoms come in waves or in hills and valleys.

You can do your best to mitigate the paranoia and delusions by limiting stress and using therapy techniques but they will always come back.

Riding out these waves, these periods of struggle gives you an extremely strong will, as well as perseverance and resiliency. With every fog that you go through you get a little better at handling it until there comes a day when the paranoia is itself a minor inconvenience.

The fact of it though, is that losing your job, getting in a car accident, breaking up with someone, these things all fall by the wayside when you've got a chronic incurable mental illness because all those things are temporary, you know that eventually you will come out of it. That realization alone takes away the power a lot of those things have to ruin a life.

Someone unaccustomed to pain will have a hell of a time while someone who's very real existence is dealing with pain everyday will look at these things and say, "So what?"

Essentially, mental illness makes people strong. Really any condition where someone has to deal with constant pain (mental or physical) will make them strong.

The point of it all is that if you are having a hard time mentally know that it's just another hill you're climbing and though there will be more, you'll eventually get to the top.

There's great strength in dealing with suffering and to be honest with you I think if you were to give me the option of having a mental illness, knowing what I know now, I wouldn't change a thing.

20

How to re-integrate into society after a major psychotic break

I was diagnosed schizophrenic in March of 2006, technically, I was diagnosed bipolar but I'll get into that later. It was after a week long, spur-of-the-moment hitchhiking trip to the U.N. thinking I was a prophet and was sent to save the world from it's various evils.

What those evils were I'm not quite sure but I knew I had a plan to unite mankind and end war. It had something to do with balance between light and dark and absolute truth, in that the ills of society were caused mostly by speculation, and if there was some absolute truth about God, the universe and everything, nobody would question anything, nobody would assume anything, everybody would understand each other on a deep spiritual level, and we could all live in perfect harmony.

Really it's nothing that countless "prophets" haven't tried to do over thousands of years, but in that moment, I was mostly unaware of religious history and thought that these answers, whatever they were, were bestowed upon me and me alone. It was up to me to fix everything.

When I finally found my way back home, thanks to a woman named Cheryl Bonner who lived somewhere in rural Massachusetts, I rambled to my parents that I was tasked with this mission and it was God's will, along with that, I'm sure some speak about aliens and conspiracies was in there too. Needless to say they were scared, so for the next seven days I was in the psychiatric ward of the Boulder Community Hospital. I wrote a book about the whole trip, fictionalized of course because God forbid I stamp the word crazy on my forehead myself.

The truth is though, I needed help, just like the four and a half percent of all adults in the United States that suffer with a serious mental illness. That equates to 14,125,500 people in these United States that suffer day in, day out, unsure of whether they can trust their own thoughts. Many recover and find help and support, but many more don't, and instead find themselves homeless or somewhere on the fringes of society where they aren't given the slightest thought, let alone assistance.
Recovery is a process.

Part and parcel of that process is learning how to re-integrate back into society and into a relative stability and normalcy. It is an extreme undertaking to achieve that normalcy and you have to want it, maybe more than anything else you've ever wanted.

When I got out of the hospital, nobody, including myself, knew what to do with me. I moved back into my parent's house and was treated with a helpless reservation. Mental illness was a foreign concept to my parents and I.

Before I broke, they thought the strange behavior was a result of marijuana and presented me with an ultimatum to either stop smoking or I would be forced out on the street. When I came home though, they regarded me with a strange silence reserved only for things they feared, and perhaps they were right to fear me, I was still very sick and dangerously delusional.

During that time I thought that every tiny action or event that took place had some incredible significance relating to me. I don't quite know how to explain it other than an intense egotism with notes of sexual discord. One example had me thinking my mom was trying to molest me when I was seated at the piano and she reached over me to the lower register, her hand brushing my lower stomach. In another instance, she caught me trying to break into the attic opening in my room, and when asked what I was doing, I told her I was looking for the treasure "they" had left me in ordaining me king or prophet or what-have-you. Those were isolated instances early on though, but I'm sure there have been others.

An integral facet of the illness, for me, was paranoia. Fear that everybody, it didn't matter who, was making fun of me, and questioning my sexuality. I'll be the first to admit that I overcompensated in that regard, trying to be as manly as possible, so some of the criticism may have been true but I can't be sure.

I was afraid to leave my house, afraid to go into stores, afraid of even ordering pizza because even the slightest interaction with someone other than my family would mean criticism and ostracism.

You can't really be sure of anything your mind tells you when you have a mental illness and the reality of that can break some people.

Many people who suffer take the course of wanting nothing to do with normalcy, instead equating the idea of recovery to something akin to drug rehab or to the idea that naturally, as their most authentic selves, they are off. It's a hard thing to accept that the way you are at your most real, is not right, and needs to be changed.
It's not a coincidence that some liken their illness to the mindset of a shaman among some remote tribe in the jungle. They can see things normal people can't, they are more spiritually in tune, they are the gateway to raw consciousness, or so they tell themselves.

They choose to embrace those things and live shunned and in some off state where they don't interact with reality, but me? I chose to be as normal as I could.

It is indeed a process to get better though, it must be maintained, and it takes some serious work. The right meds are key, and therapy is key, but the extreme side-effects that go along with the meds harden folks. People with mental illness are some of the most resilient and courageous people there are. They don't pretend to be someone they aren't, warts and demonic voices and all. That raw authenticity can scare people and I can see why.

What's their reward for such strength though? Going years after diagnosis cycling through myriad different med combinations and therapy techniques in hopes that they can find something that works, or at the very least, something they can tolerate. If they find that combination, life is ok, and ok really is the best they can ask.

What was originally thought to be bipolar disorder, my diagnosis, and may have been complicated by certain meds, was changed to schizoaffective disorder, and then schizophrenia with periods of depression by a good doctor named Dr. Wenoker. A quiet man I worked with for six years who may just be the best in the business.

About a year after diagnosis, I somehow managed to get a job as a reporter at newspaper in a small mountain town covering local news and city council meetings, but knowing nothing about journalism aside from the two years in journalism school before I dropped out due to my illness, I really had no idea what I was doing and what I was supposed to do. In my inexperienced unwillingness to devote myself to an endlessly monotonous series of city council meetings, and trying to find something interesting enough to write about, I lost the job and floundered living off what remained of my college savings and the goodwill of my parents.

It took me two years after diagnosis to find a med combination that worked on my mind, sadly though, it didn't work with my body. I gained about 100 pounds, took up smoking and was too tired most days to get out of bed in the morning. In that time there were hints of recovery but they didn't last long. Dr. Wenoker was actually more receptive to the complications than I was and adjusted my meds with great care when the need arose. With his help I lost the weight and regained a hint of stability.

Also in that time, my parents began to come to terms with my illness, attending support groups and integrating themselves into the mental illness community in Colorado.

They spent the better part of those years immersing themselves in the bureaucracy of finding me government assistance. Endless applications and appeal processes later, they found me an apartment in government housing. I like to think living in the projects for a year gives me street cred, but, really, it's just sad.
Boulder's projects are actually pretty nice too, considering. It took several years and three or four application processes for anything else though. When the applications and appeals began to get accepted, things started looking up and before I knew it I was awarded section 8 housing, which meant I could pick where I lived, as long as they accepted section 8.

I would be lying if I didn't say some of the properties out there that cater to the disabled community aren't much better and many times worse than actual projects in Chicago and the like, but who am I to comment?

I found a small one-bedroom in a tiny town called Niwot down the highway from Boulder, which was possibly one of the best section 8 properties out there, so I consider myself fortunate. A year into my time in Niwot, I was awarded food stamp benefits and social security and disability income, which has been barely enough to get by but it keeps food in my stomach, meds in my brain and cigarettes in my mouth and that's fine for right now, but I'm always working for more.

In my seven years living with schizophrenia there have been periods of relative stability where I questioned if I really had any illness but, in some small part, those times have always been marred by one constant arc that reminds me everyday that I'm still sick; that being the paranoia. It's the continuing fear that people were making fun of me. It's hard to live normally under a veil of fear, it impacts relationships, interactions, and behavior. I've had to learn to avoid situations that cause me paranoia. Pretty much any situation in which interacting with other people is a requisite has been hard for me to accept. I've even found crutches like being introverted and reclusiveness to help me with that but I know it can't last and I'm slowly making my way forward.

In my worst times, though, I think I hear conversations about my sexuality and I think the laughter I hear behind me is about me. Suffice it to say, I have trust issues.

Perhaps even more of a curse was dealing with the stigma of having a mental illness. When's the right time to tell a girl you're dating or a casual acquaintance that you had a psychotic break and were diagnosed schizophrenic? Major mental illnesses are chronic, they stick with you for life. There is no cure for mental illness and the label alone can break someone.

The media hasn't helped in portraying mental illness as something to fear, citing the emotional and psychological problems of people who cause harm to others through violence.

After a major story on some massacre one can be sure that there will be a piece following closely that discusses how the killer was a quiet man, who kept to himself and has said some strange things or exhibited some strange behavior in the past.

Endless studies have shown that people with major mental illness are much more likely to be victims of senseless crimes than to be perpetrators, but society has painted us differently.

 Maybe it's up to me, and articles like this to change minds. I hope they do.

Things are ok now, I'm stable, I have good health care and a good family who watch out for me and the semblance of a career, but there seems to be a period or two every year where things fall apart, I get more paranoid, more delusional, fall into a depression, consider ending things, and in some way it all comes to a head. I'll either post something worrying on Facebook or say some strange thing to my parents, which, in the last seven years they've learned to recognize as a red flag. The next couple months after that are usually marked by an increase in meds and maybe a complication or two with side-effects and then slowly, and with a lot of rest on my part, and a lot of patience on my family's part, that relative ok-ness.

I've gotten better at interacting with people too. It takes some serious work though. I've read endless books on social psychology, body language, dating and pretty much anything you can think of having to do with social interaction and although they teach me things, there's no substitute for practice.

The true cure for paranoia though, is self-assurance, and the only way someone can get that self-assurance is intense and radical acceptance of the things they fear, their faults and everything that makes them wonder about themselves. I needed to be ok with the idea that people may have been making fun of me, that they may have been questioning my sexuality, and the very real possibility that I may in fact, have been gay for me to be ok with myself and find that self assurance. Just so you know, and if it matters at all, I still like girls, I've never not liked girls, I was just very confused there for a while.

Truthfully though, questioning one's identity is a necessary part of growing up, and I'm still not entirely convinced that it's a coincidence most major mental illnesses present themselves in someone's early twenties, a time when people are just beginning to figure out who they truly are.

As for a conclusion, and as for how to re-integrate into society after a major mental illness, If you want to be normal, you need to take your meds everyday, you need to go to therapy, and you need to take an active role in your own recovery. Just like anything that's worth doing, it takes an immense amount of work and some people aren't cut out for it.

Dealing at once, with the intense confusion, delusions, paranoia as well as the social implications of having the crazy label is an intense, and not to be overlooked undertaking.

These people are stronger than you will ever know and to shun them and treat them with fear is something that speaks to the essence of one's character. If you can, try not to do it. The only thing we really want is respect and a chance at a normal life.

We are not monsters, we're just trying to get well.

21

On Seeing Others Who Are Suffering

As someone with a disability, there are times in my week
when I'm faced with the inevitable sentence of my diagnosis.
These times are marked by moments when I can tell
something isn't right with my thinking. Over the last seven
years I've developed a skill for noticing these glitches and
when they occur, I'm equipped with years worth of therapy
techniques and a healthy dose of antipsychotic medication to
help deal with them. I'm aware an existence subdued by these
myriad techniques and medications doesn't quite sound like it
would be a good one to live but, to that, I'll say, I didn't ask
for this shit but I do what I can to not let it bother me, and if a
lifelong regimen of meds and therapy techniques is what can
guarantee a relative peace, well, I can adapt.

Also inherent in my sentence is an empathy not seen by most.
I can tell just by a quick glance if someone is dealing with
some not so good stuff, or is suffering some ill that isn't fair.
Suffering is marked, more often than not, by a chin kept up, in
essence, a not entirely real confidence.

They have a way about them, perhaps more sarcastic than necessary, a quick wit and a fierce resistance to being fucked with. Many times, their fingertips are marked by a yellowing from too many cigarettes and uncut nails because fuck personal hygiene. They usually wear large sunglasses that cover a good majority of their face, and if they are a man, they will have a beard and a ball cap in combination with the aforementioned sunglasses. Anything to create a relative distance from the world and give them a place to hide. They have attitude, they wear leather jackets, play in bands with explicit sexual innuendos as names, drink entirely too much and at the apex of everything, they rebel. They simply will not be told how to live their lives.

On the extreme end of the spectrum, the attitude is gone, replaced entirely by an intense apathy. There will be no regard for fashion or hygiene, they will wear the clothes their caretakers picked up at a thrift shop, not because it's trendy or ironic but because that's all they could afford on their government assistance. Their hair will be long and unkempt because to bother anyone with a severe mental illness with doing more in a day than getting out of bed and smoking a few cigarettes is unfair. These are the people to whom life is the most cruel. They exist only because they have to and because they know that someone somewhere, be it just their mother or father, cares about them enough. Life isn't life for these people, it is simply a succession of days into nights spent wondering why things are the way they are and waiting for the soft cocoon of their warm beds every night which offer them their only escape.

It hurts my soul to see people who are suffering that way. I want to do something for them and to elevate them to a place where they can feel at least a fleeting sense of comfort but I can't. I don't know what to do for them. I've told my loved ones when I was going through some dark periods that the best thing they can do for me is to simply be with me and let me know they're there and that, I think, is what suffering people need the most, to know that they're not alone.

Here's the sad part though, as much as I want to help these people, I also vehemently don't. To involve myself in that level suffering only reminds me of the illness I deal with everyday. Sure I may be farther along in recovery than most of these people but to confront the truth of what severe mental illness can do to a person is, to say the least, deeply uncomfortable. It's the reason you lock your doors when a shady figure approaches your car, it's the reason you look away from the character that stands outside your apartment building smoking, it's the reason you don't give change to the man standing on the street corner with a cardboard sign.

These people are the undesirables, the people you silently judge without giving it a second thought. They exist and you know that but you will, by hook or by crook stay as far away from them as possible.
Like it or not, the people you want to stay far away from are the people that need the most help. They are the ones who've lost the most and who exist simply to survive. Ironically, these are the people who also have the most courage because they've seen the absolute bottom of the barrel. Some are able to pull themselves out, some aren't.

I will say that there's a strange disconnect in somebody like me who avoids these people, but at the same time, realizes that, inherently, with every fiber of my being, whether I like it or not, I am one of these people.

The only difference between me and them is that I realized
that that way of life wasn't something I wanted for myself so I
worked my ass off to become as normal and everyday as I
could.

Some say, when I tell them about my illness that they can't
even tell, and I won't lie, although I never stop pushing
myself to that ideal, it feels good when someone can't tell
because that means I've made it back to the land of the living.

I feel sorry for those who suffer everyday but if you do the
things your doctor recommends and fight for the ideal
everyday of your life, you can find a relative normalcy.

I'll say this, maybe we're not afraid of these people because
they are the lowest rung but because they have the most
courage and we can see that and it scares us because we know
we could never deal with the hand they've been dealt.

22

<u>How to Trick People Into Thinking You're Normal</u>

I was diagnosed with schizophrenia when I was twenty years old. It developed slowly at first with strange notions that my friends didn't understand me and had some agenda against me. I thought I was brilliant and I was keyed into something that nobody else was privy to. I struggled with the notion that nobody understood me and the significance of things for some time, all the while, I was smoking generous amounts of pot and was becoming increasingly paranoid.

Things broke altogether on some week night in my freshman year of college when a dorm hall mate made some inane comment while we were smoking weed, that, in truth, meant nothing significant, but to me it was the worst thing anyone could have ever said. It shook my existence and I went back to my room and lost my shit. There was a warm pain in my head and I could feel my mind splitting in two. It was an innocent and insecure jab that utterly broke me.
Every day after, I was terrified to leave my room. It took every ounce of strength I had to leave and attempt to go to class. On my best days I made it through one class before the alerts in my head were too much to bear and I had to go back to my room to hopefully sleep the paranoia off.

Before long the semester was over and I came home.

I existed in this warm pain for the better part of two years never going farther than the grocery store or class when I had the wherewithal to go. It hurt to be in public and I, with my two minds, was experiencing the world tangibly with one, and analytically with the other. I was in tune if you can call it that; to an incredibly high degree. People's deepest insecurities were revealed to me through their walk, their expressions, their tones of voice. I could read people, but at the same time, I was terrified that they were reading me and judging me just as harshly.

Now I don't need to tell you guys this, but that's not normally the best way to function as a human being.
I'm pretty sure I'm not a psychopath because I feel deeply for those who struggle, but being incredibly paranoid about what other people are thinking of you, should probably have a place reserved for it pretty far up on the egotistical scale.

In this paranoia, nobody can be sure how to act.
Especially when it comes to the idea of pleasing others with your incredibly authentic looking, yet entirely fake way of interacting with the world, put on simply so you can pretend to be a normal member of society and not be outwardly freaking out and completely overwhelmed by how the world perceives you every second of every minute of every hour.

For those of you struggling with being a normal functioning member of society and not some raving lunatic I've put together a helpful guide to help you at least trick people into thinking you're normal, hopefully if you follow these steps you'll actually start to become normal. Granted I'm still struggling with this but you know what they say, "fake it 'til you make it."

1. Spend several years floundering while at the same time studying and analyzing every single interaction you have from hours hanging out with close friends to the 30 second period of small talk you have while handing your money to the pizza delivery man. Notice not only levels of eye contact, but also body language and the way people carry themselves. If you get good at it, you'll not only have a good baseline to incorporate into your behavior patterns but you'll also start to recognize when people are struggling on their own with this stuff. Most importantly repeat to yourself day after day, no matter how paranoid about it you are, that nobody really cares how you act beyond a shallow and base surface notion about how you're kind of quirky.

2. Read every book you can get your hands on about human interaction, from manuals by former spies on body language, to books about the deeper levels of neuroscience examining social structure and why we act the way we do on a biological level, to books by the pick-up community about manipulative ways to act in order to get girls to like you. If you're lucky, you'll realize that no matter what you read none of that stuff matters in everyday practice.

3. Become overwhelmed by it all and refuse to leave your house for a period of no less than a month during which time you cement your status as a recluse and effectively get your friends to stop inviting you anywhere because they know you're not going to come.

4. Explore and experiment with different facets of personality that give you an excuse for acting the way you do from being an introvert to, being a psychopath, to being reclusive writer to being a serial killer. Notice all the parallels between the way these people act and the way you act, and wonder if you effectively fit into any of those categories. Realize you don't and become depressed that you can't find a way to classify yourself aside from being mentally ill.

5. Over the course of several years, become really good at faking it, like really really good, to the point where people feel comfortable around you. They'll still feel like there's some missing point though, something that doesn't quite make sense about you, something that's just a tiny bit off. If you've gotten good enough to alleviate that notion on their part though, you'll still be paranoid about it for yourself and work relentlessly to be normal or to fit into other people's idea of being normal.

6. Lose hope altogether and resort to therapy until it makes you question the very basis of who you are then stop going because it makes you uncomfortable.

7. Take your meds and continue increasing the dose until you are either to dopey to care or too blank to realize what's going on. Be comfortable.

8. Lose it again when something stressful happens and start the cycle again, this time though, you're more prepared for it even though it hurts just as much as it ever has.

9. Realize what you learned in therapy was right to a degree and accept your faults. Instead of trying relentlessly to fit into something or somewhere through the way you act. Just give up the fight and accept that you may not ever be normal. Accept your quirks and your paranoia as a reality and not something that should be hidden. Also accept that there are people out there who wish to classify you and judge you whether you like it or not and that is nothing more than a passive-aggressive attempt on their part to get you to notice them. I've found that, not only do I feel the most normal when I'm ok with and I accept the way things are, I also feel like people treat me the most normal. Everyone has faults and if you try desperately to hide them from the world, people will only start to suspect something.

10. Be relatively ok.

23

How to Feel Good

If you're anything like me you're in your late twenties with a patchy beard, a dislike of wearing shoes you have to tie the laces of, a growing affinity towards clothing that makes you feel comfortable as opposed to stylish and last but not least a seething, gnawing jadedness and mistrust of the world and all the shitty people that despite never having met, you just get that feeling they'd suck to know.

The last year of my life has been marked by a relative paranoia of the outside world followed closely by a depression that things were never going to change. There was the feeling that every person besides myself, and my immediate family had the express intention of blocking my shots, slamming doors in my face and finding any and every opportunity to find something wrong with me and criticize it openly, or just out of earshot.

In a few words, it was me against the world, and although I never gave up and broke down, except for one vaguely suicidal over-sharing Facebook status on my part. Still I woke every day and fought until I went to bed at 7:30 pm because I just couldn't fucking take any more and my only respite was sleep and the land of dreams.

That said, during that time I employed every tactic I had ever come across to combat my dissatisfaction from therapy to cognitive behavioral techniques to positive affirmations and finally, gasp, to praying to a god I was pretty sure didn't even exist.

Still, talking and analyzing and exploring moods can only do so much when you have a chronic illness of the mind. I've read other articles bashing prescription brain drugs here as having serious and scary side effects, anywhere from increased depression to weird sleepwalking to weight gain to suicidal tendencies. That's all fine and good, but in truth, psychopharmacology is the only thing that's really ever worked for me.

Mental health providers are divided on their approaches to treating serious mental conditions, and to be honest the whole thing really is a sort of crap shoot, hell they don't even have hard methods to diagnose it, aside from a series of questionnaires and initial consultations.

All I know is that I'll do anything not to feel shitty, paranoid and delusional and if that includes taking pills that have been to shown to reduce the life expectancy of someone talking them by 20 or 30 years, I'm doing it.

Honestly, I've been ready to go to the great beyond since my first major episode. It'd be a hell of a lot easier not to have to feel things and to just put an end to it. Mental illness is a tough mother to deal with every day.

I can remember back when I was in the hospital among seven or eight other severely delusional people and they all wanted to know why I willingly took my pills while they all chose to spit them out. I hesitate to say I was smarter or more clear headed than them but I had come to the distinct realization that by taking my pills, going to daily therapy and doing the act the doctors expected of me, I would only get out of that hell hole sooner.

The thing is, I also realized that I felt better when I took the pills and the thoughts that scared the hell out of me, even if just a little, seemed to quiet down.

For anyone that's been on the other side of the mental illness fence, sleepwalking and a little weight gain are puny compared to the prospect of not feeling straight out of your fucking mind, ready to rip out your fucking hair every minute of every hour of every day.

The funny thing about antipsychotics is that they lower the amount of dopamine and seratonin in your brain. So if you are a normally mentally functioning person that somehow has the pleasure of taking them, of course you're gonna have a shitty time.

For us who have way too much of these feel good chemicals in our brain the effects of antipsychotics are only going to help. After all, everything in moderation right?

Now that I've said all that, I'll get to the part of the article that you all came here for, how to feel good.
Truth is, I don't know.

I do know that I felt pretty good last night after an intimate dinner with some old friends that I haven't seen in a while. We ate, and discussed things in comfortable chairs in front of a fire. There was a general feeling that, for once, in however long, I was doing it right. I was being accepted by these people, and I felt a way I haven't felt in a long time, relaxed, maybe even happy.

That, and I've been making progress with a certain girl, which after years of rejection and missteps on my part on the path towards potential relationships, feels really fucking good. She may even like me, which is always a plus.

So maybe that's the answer, good friends, good food, a fire, and the potential of love, and if you're in the mental illness camp like me, some good meds may help too.

After all, to feel relaxed and happy is pretty much all we can ask for right?

24

How to put the brakes on if you're feeling overwhelmed

A lot of people run through their lives going from one task to another without taking time to stop and smell the roses.

Our society is overworked, and as result, overstressed.

I know what it's like to get so overwhelmed on something that you slowly start to lose your grip on reality. That's just one of the many things I have to deal with living with schizophrenia.

The point is, it's important to put the brakes when you start to feel overwhelmed. This is just as important for regular people as it is for people with a major mental illness but I won't lie and say that these two types of people react to stress the same way.

Putting the brakes on is difficult too and I'd venture to guess that are a good amount of people out there who work so hard that they've lost track of how exactly to go about doing it.

I think the first thing you need to remember is that whatever the task is, it can be broken into chunks. Essentially this means setting small goals for yourself and taking time out in the in-between periods after you've accomplished one part but have yet to get to another.

I'll be honest, the reason I'm writing this article is as much for your benefit as it is for mine. Currently I have the major task of rewriting my first book for an agent, updating my posts here on PsychCentral and continuing to do articles for the New York Times hanging over my head and I've noticed that in the last few weeks my mood has been more sour than usual, I have an increased amount of paranoia and I'm feeling a little depressed.

I as much as anybody need to be conscious of my health and that means getting a handle on my stress.

That said, what do I know about stress?

I know that I need to take it easy from time to time and my preferred way of taking it easy is going for walks and losing myself in some good music. I know that I need to do these things to maintain my stability as a person living with a mental illness and I know that sometimes I forget.

Whatever your form of stress relief is, do it. If it helps, try even scheduling your chill out time into your calendar. That way, you don't have to feel bad about not getting anything done.

Another major thing that helps me is rewarding myself for a job well done. This essentially ties into breaking down massive tasks into more manageable chunks. Once you do a small chunk don't feel guilty about letting your hair down for a little while. Celebrate the fact that you've made progress.

Sometimes it's going for a walk, sometimes it's going out for a good meal, and sometimes it's just sitting on your couch and watching a good movie.

It's important though.
Another good trick is looking forward to your schedule and working to relieve some of the burden that lies ahead. If you have to say no to a project for your mental health, you have to say no. Don't be afraid to do what you need to do to lighten the load.

The main thing to remember is that stress is not a good thing to deal with, it's so easy to lose yourself in it but taking the time and the actions you need to take in order to maintain a good level of stability is perfectly acceptable.

Nobody is going to fault you for being conscious about your health.

25

Delusions of Grandeur: Can One Person Really Affect Society?

I like to think I'm important. I may not be of relative importance to my city or my community but I like to think that, to the people I care about, I mean something.

I've strived for lofty goals and to get recognized as a writer and photographer in myriad ways and I've always hoped that my life, or the actions I take in my life, contributed something meaningful to the world.

At times, thanks to mental illness, I've even thought that I was the be-all-end-all example of ideal behavior and that my actions were being watched and scrutinized by the entire world to the point of absurdity.

A delusion of grandeur is defined by Google's native definition software as "a delusion (common in paranoia) that you are much greater and more powerful and influential than you really are."

A common thread in most stories of psychotic breaks is the delusion that the person involved was either, God himself, Jesus Christ, a prophet, a king, or even the President of the United States.

The notion that their paranoia of being watched escalated to the point where they thought that it was true, and further, the deduction that the only reason they would be being watched so carefully must be that they are of crucial importance, is extremely prevalent amongst the schizophrenic community. It's a notion that exists or has existed at some point in most of these people's minds and many times it shapes their recovery and the type of person they develop into after their first episode.

Schizophrenia aside, the question stands, does one unknown person's behavior actually have any real affect on society or even their own community?

Thanks to the internet and social media, influence can be measured in metrics like the amount of followers one has, or how many times their content has been shared and commented on.

There are even a selection of websites and services online dedicated to analysis and improvement of social media influence. One particular service called 'Klout' gives a numerical score of your social media influence.
"The Klout Score measures a person's overall online influence on a scale of one to 100, with 100 being the most influential. Klout's system analyzes variables across multiple social networks based on your engagement." –Klout.com

Still though, does any of that really matter or have any lasting effect?

In my quest for a relative peace of mind I've found myself living in small towns and cities alike. In each, a sense of relative community can be entirely different.

As far as small towns go, if you've ever lived in one for a significant amount of time, you know that sometimes, the familiar faces become a little too familiar. These faces become your community whether you like it or not. Sometimes there are things that you'd rather not share with these people but in the midst of all that, notions are formed and notions turn to speculation and speculation turns to gossip and for anyone on the receiving end of gossip, it can be suffocating.

That's when the idea to move to a city forms.

"Gotta get away from these people, gotta move to a place where I won't know anyone and where I can blend in and be as anonymous as I choose."

However, once one moves to the city, they find themselves in the worst kind of lonely, isolated amongst thousands of people.

The same can be said of a social media reputation. Twitter and Tumblr are the big cities and Facebook is, and always will be, the small town.

Perhaps you've over-shared on Facebook one two many times, gotten into a heated and schizophrenic argument with anonymous talking heads on twitter, or in the case of the movie and resulting MTV show Catfish and The Manti Te'o scandal, maybe you've just pretended to be the wrong person.

One could even argue that a stagnant online reputation is the catalyst for people to take on fake identities online in the first place, they want something different, but, in the words of Bob Marley "Ya running and ya running and ya running away... But ya can't run away from yourself." If only they would realize the consequences their actions would take on any reputation small morsel of reputation they had left.

In a city, small town or online, the rules of social engagement maybe tighter or looser but the fact remains that they are still extremely present and, without regard, will rule the dynamics on which life on a social scale exists.

If you spend enough time observing and analyzing this social engagement both online and off you will, without question, see patterns start to emerge. Each community has it's own patterns just as each social network has it's own patterns.

These patterns seem to be inherent with any sort of social engagement. They are, simply, required as part of a social reality. They are the rules that govern how people act and they are present in both real life and the darkest depths of the seediest internet forums.

There's a way one is supposed to act, regardless of circumstances, and if you deviate, your membership to both on and offline social groups may suffer.

Of course each of the patterns in social situations carry nuances, and each person chooses to carry out these patterns with their own personal nuances or idiosyncrasies, most usually, the ones they've grown up realizing work for a given situation.

For someone like me though, who analyzes these patterns and nuances so intently, one starts to notice that the nuances they struggle with the most, (the awkwardness of poor timing, the self manifesting insecurities, and the lack of distinct rhythm of personality) seem to cause a significant amount of struggle for other people as well.

In times like that, and this may be a delusion of grandeur, one starts to wonder whether their own personal discord was somehow translated through their actions, movements, interactions, or nuances and whether others are watching and analyzing them just as intently for social cues on either the positive or negative.

Are these other people picking up your discord? Do they look to you for the correct social cues like you look to them? If so, are you even performing the correct social cues? Further, what exactly are the correct social cues for any given situation?
Most importantly, does what you do affect the way they will act in the future?
Do others incorporate your social failings and insecurities into their own patterns?
This question seems to be equally valid both online and offline.

"An errant spark can set a forest aflame" "Be the change you want to see in this world" We've heard these quotes or iterations on the themes in them from political leaders, "masters" and spiritual gurus alike but do they really mean anything?

Change and effect takes followers and in the words of Derek Sivers, in his TED talk 'How to Start a Movement' "The first follower is actually an underestimated form of leadership, in itself. It takes guts to stand out like that. The first follower is what transforms a lone nut into a leader"

Twitter and Tumblr are both prime examples of this leader-follower dynamic. Those who have the most followers also have the greatest amount of influence.

For a simpleton like me though who has less than 100 followers, one wonders, who exactly are these followers and are we leading a movement we don't know about simply by existing and acting the way we do anonymously?

It's clear to see that celebrities, politicians, innovators, and people of influence have some power in the social cue regard. Consequently, these are also the people who have the most followers on any social network and their influence online is just as great as any influence they have in their own communities. If they do things correctly, or the way society deems correctly, they are looked up to and lauded as role models, but if they divert from expected behavior, they are chided and ridiculed and their reputation may be permanently damaged.

One need only look to the allegations of abuse and twitter rants of Chris Brown, to the infamous shaving of Britney Spears' head, or to the undercover doping operation of Lance Armstrong (all people once revered for their talent) to see that errant social behavior can kill, not only a reputation, but also a brand. Especially online, where things like this can be shared rapidly.

At the same time, perfection in work and social engagement can build a reputation from nothing, and not only affect a society, but change it for the better.

Look at innovators in oratory skills like President Obama, or innovators in technology like Steve Jobs.

They each demand perfection in their public involvement, though their private lives may be another matter, they have effectively created a pinnacle for leadership. They never make a social misstep and their followers reward them by listening, intently.

Innovators aside, the question remains. Can one, relatively unknown person's behavior have any effect on society?

I'd venture to say yes, granted they position themselves in a role of leadership. I'd also venture to say that everyone, no matter who it is, is going to find themselves in at least one or two roles of leadership during their time on planet earth. People will look up to and admire someone who has social grace, confidence and an air of leadership and everyone, regardless of who they are, is an expert in something. They will have their time to shine.

As to the effects on a person that consistently projects that air, and never falters or shows weakness because it's required of them, one need only click through the slideshows that come out every four years showing how the president, whoever he or she is, has aged during their time in office.

Be it even the dead-eyed crack addict who rides the subway everyday because he has nowhere else to go, everyone has an influence on the people they encounter, even if just for a moment. The proof of this statement lies in the warm feeling one gets after a particularly rough week and the simple sweet smile of a well-meaning stranger that just seems to make everything better.

We most definitely have an affect on the people we love. Their way of being is incorporated into us whether we like it or not. We are parts of them, just as they are parts of us.

As far as our insecurities though, the things we don't want to project and the things we don't want to have much of an influence, well, they do, just, thankfully, not to the degree we worry about.

It would be a weird and confusing world if every person we encountered was analyzing us, and our nuances, as vigorously as we analyze ourselves.

What strangers think and feel about us, and the way we act is their own business.

How we see the world versus how they may see it lies at the core question of humanity and what it means to live in a world populated by other people who are not ourselves. It's a question that defines culture and is the very essence of right vs. wrong: how do we treat other people?

We can only strive to be the best versions of ourselves and treat others the way we'd like to be treated. This is true whether we're online or not.

That said, no matter who you are, it probably is best that you, in the words of Napoleon Hill, "Think twice before you speak, because your words and influence will plant the seed of either success or failure in the mind of another"